# God Brings Life Out Of Adversity

## Joann Berkhouse

# PREFACE

THIS COLLECTION OF POEMS IS MY JOURNEY FROM DEALING WITH THE PROBLEMS, STRUGGLES AND HEARTACHES IN MY LIFE TO LEARNING GOD'S HAND IS EVER PRESENT IN OUR LIVES. EVEN WHEN, WE CAN'T SEE HIS LOVE AND COMPASSION, THROUGH THE DARK CLOUDS THAT SURROUND US. HE SAID IN THE BIBLE THAT HE WOULD NEVER LEAVE OR FORSAKE HIS CHILDREN.

I WANT TO THANK GOD FOR GIVING ME THE INSPIRATION AND MOTIVATION TO WRITE THESE SELECTIONS AND GET THEM IN A FORM THAT YOU (MY READERS) COULD GET SOME CONSOLATION AND HOPE FROM THEM.

THERE ARE MANY PEOPLE WHO HAVE HELPED ME MAKE THIS LITTLE BOOK A REALITY. FOREMOST ARE MY DAUGHTERS, SUSANNE AND ANITA, WHO HAVE WALKED THIS JOURNEY WITH ME, HAVE MOTIVATED ME AND BEEN AMAZING DAUGHTERS. MY LATE HUSBAND, RICHARD, WHO I FEEL IS CHEERING US ON FROM GLORY AND, WHILE HERE, DID ALL IN HIS POWER TO LOVE, PROVIDE AND SUPPORT US.

I CAN'T SAY ENOUGH THANKS TO JUDITH, MY NIECE, WHOSE REMARKABLE ARTISTIC TALENT, DISPLAYED THROUGHOUT THIS BOOK, TRULY, SPURRED ME ON TO THE COMPLETION OF THIS PROJECT.

CAROL, SONNIE, KAREN, KATHY, CAROLE, SHANNON AND ROBERTA HAVE LISTENED TO MY COMPLAINTS, DISAPPOINTMENTS AND REGRETS, WHILE REJOICING WITH ME IN THE GOOD TIMES THROUGH THE YEARS. THEY HAVE ENCOURAGED ME TO KEEP WALKING ON AND NOT TO LOOK BACK. I TREASURE ALL OF MY FAMILY AND FRIENDS WITHOUT WHOM, I QUESTION WHERE I WOULD BE TODAY. I ALSO THANK GOD FOR LEADING ME TO MY NEW FRIEND, MICHAEL, WHO HAS BEEN SO GRACIOUS HELPING THIS WORK TO BE PUBLISHED.

I PRAY YOU WILL GLEAN HOPE, BLESSING AND JOY, AS YOU READ.

## TABLE OF CONTENTS

## I PRAY

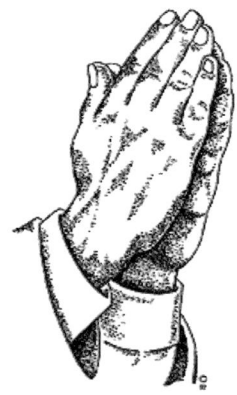

I PRAY THE POEMS
IN THIS LITTLE BOOK
BLESSES YOU WITH INSIGHT
AS YOU TAKE A LOOK
AT SOMEONE ELSE'S PROBLEMS
TO SEE HOW THEY WERE BLESSED
OR FOUND A WAY TO HANDLE
A STRUGGLE OR A TEST.

WE HAVE THE OPPORTUNITY
TO BE A GUIDING LIGHT;
FOR SOMEONE, WHO IS STRUGGLING
IN A SOUL'S DARK NIGHT.
WHEN HOPES AND DREAMS ARE SHATTERED
PERHAPS GOD HAS ANOTHER PLAN.
HOPE CAN BE REBORN AGAIN
IF WE LEAVE THINGS IN GOD'S HANDS.

OUR LIVES ARE INTERTWINED
AS WE JOURNEY ON OUR WAY;
WITH MESSAGES OF HOPE
AND ANSWERS WHEN WE PRAY.
THINGS WILL BE MORE CLEAR
WHEN WE LISTEN TO HIS VOICE.
BLESSINGS WILL COME OUR WAY
OBEYING WILL BE OUR CHOICE.

## THE WINTER OF MY LIFE

LOOKING OUT MY WINDOW
AT THE COLD AND HARSH I SEE
A PRISONER OF THE WEATHER
MY HEART WOULD GLADLY FLEE.

FOUR WALLS GROWING SMALLER;
BREATH, SOMETIMES HARD TO FIND,
I'M SITTING IN MY SOLITUDE
AS SNOW AND ICE COLLIDE.

SUNSHINE WOULD BE WELCOME
TO CHASE AWAY THE GLOOM.
JUST NEEDING SOME ADVENTURE
AND ESCAPING FROM MY ROOM.

DREAMING OF SPRING FLOWERS
OR A WARM SUMMER NIGHT
WITH A STAR-STUDDED SKY
WOULD BE A DELIGHT.

BUT ALL THINGS CAN BE BLESSINGS
EVEN THIS COLD WINTER TIME.
BEING THANKFUL FOR WHAT GOD GIVES
FROM HIS HAND DIVINE.

I KNOW THE SEASONS CHANGE.
GOD'S SUN WILL LIGHT THE WAY.
THIS TIME I'M LIVING SOON WILL PASS.
SUNSHINE WILL COME ANOTHER DAY.

## OUR DAYS

THE STORY OF OUR DAYS
AS OUR FEET GO NEAR AND FAR
AND THE CHOICES OF OUR LIVES
MAKE UP WHO WE ARE.

ECHOES OF SAD TIMES,
OF LAUGHTER AND TEARS
SWEEP O'ER MY MEMORIES,
MY PARADE OF YEARS.

THE GRAY OF MY TRIALS
AND WRINKLES FROM TEARS
MESH WITH MY DREAMS,
MY HOPES AND MY FEARS.

MEMORIES OF FUN DAYS
AS BUTTERFLIES FLIT BY,
SUN-FILLED AND HAPPY
LIKE CLOUDS IN THE SKY.

SMILING INSTEAD OF CRYNG
CAN CHASE BLUES AWAY;
AND SOON COMES THE SUNSHINE
TO FACE ANOTHER DAY.

## DARKNESS-HOPE

DARKNESS SURROUNDS ME.
BREATHING IS NIL.
HAPPINESS ALLUDES ME.
ALL ABOUT ME IS STILL.

IT IS, OH, SO COLD
CLEAR TO THE HEART
FROM THIS DREARY PRISON
I NEED TO DEPART.

A HOPE FOR THE FUTURE
APPEARS TO BE DIM.
MY DREAM OF SUNSHINE
SEEMS TO BE SLIM.

TIME IS NOT MY FRIEND.
IT SEEMS TO CREEP ALONG;
WAITING SEEMS FOREVER
WHILE TRYING TO BE STRONG.

WHAT IS THIS I SENSE,
MOVEMENT, I FEEL WITHIN?
A STIRRING OF EMOTIONS
IS TRYING TO BEGIN.

GOD HAS FINALLY HEARD.
MY CRY HAS REACHED HIS EARS.
I'VE NOT BEEN FORGOTTEN;
HE FELT ALL MY FEARS.

I'VE BROKEN THROUGH THE DIRT.
MY SOUL HAS FOUND RELEASE.
GOD'S OPENED UP MY HEART
AND GIVEN ME HIS PEACE.

## STOP AND LISTEN

IS YOUR HEART HEAVY?
SO YOU WANT TO CRY;
BUT, THE TEARS WON'T COME
AND YOU DON'T KNOW, WHY?

ARE CIRCUMSTANCES PRESSING
TO LIMITS OF DESPAIR?
DO YOU SOMETIMES WONDER
WHY TO, EVEN, CARE?

IF DAYS SEEM TO HAVE NO VALUE
AND SLEEPLESS NIGHTS INCREASE;
KNOW THERE IS AN ANSWER -
A PLACE TO FIND RELEASE.

THE ANSWER IS SO SIMPLE.
IT'S BURIED IN THE NEED
AND HAS TO BE UNCOVERED;
IT'S LETTING THE LORD LEAD.

YOU SEE, THE KEY'S SO SIMPLE.
STOP AND LISTEN TO HIS VOICE.
GOD HAS THE ANSWER WAITING
BUT, WE MUST MAKE THE CHOICE.

HE WANTS TO GIVE US BLESSINGS
AND SHOW US WHERE TO GO,
MAKE OUR LIVES WORTHWHILE
AND CLOSER TO HIM, GROW.

## WILDERNESS

THERE COME TIMES IN OUR LIVES
WE SEEM TO BE SET APART;
A TIME WHEN THE WORLD SEEMS SO DARK
AND GOD, TO REACH IS NOUGHT.

IT SEEMS A CHORE, EVEN, TO BREATHE
WHILE KNOWING WHAT'S BEEN TAUGHT.
DEEP IN THE HEART, YOU KNOW IT'S TRUE,
THAT YOUR SOUL, CHRIST HAS BOUGHT.

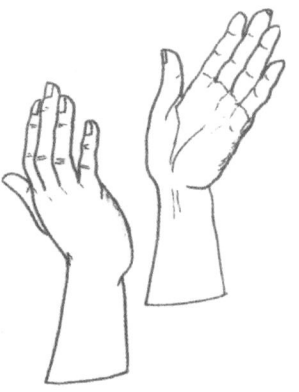

HIS CREATION REMAINS AND CONTINUES ON
THROUGH SPRING, SUMMER, WINTER, FALL.
AT TIMES, YOU WONDER WHY YOU'RE HERE
REACHING FOR HEAVEN, BUT FINDING A WALL.

A WEB OF QUESTIONS, DOUBTS AND FEARS
KEEP ARISING IN YOUR MIND.
BUT, HOLDING ON AND TRUSTING GOD,
THE PEACE OF GOD, YOU'LL FIND.

FROM FEAR, YOU'LL BE DELIVERED
AS FAITH GROWS, IN TIME, GREATER.
REST IN HIS LOVE AND KNOW HE CARES;
YOUR PATH WILL THEN BE STRAIGHTER.

JUST REACH OUT TO THE LORD.
THERE IS NO OTHER WAY.
HE'LL ALWAYS BE TRUE TO HIS WORD;
HE'S THERE FOR YOU EVERY DAY.

## THROUGH MY PROBLEMS

I WILL PRAISE YOU THROUGH MY PROBLEMS
AND  WHEN I FEEL NO HOPE;
EVEN WHEN CIRCUMSTANCES FIND ME
AT THE END OF MY ROPE.

AT MY MESS, I WILL NOT LOOK
OR SEE WITH EYES OF CLAY;
BUT, WITH THE FAITH OF HEAVEN,
MY EYES, ON JESUS STAY.

LET NOT YOUR HEART BE TROUBLED
AND GIVE IT ALL TO HIM
ARE WHAT I NEED TO REMEMBER
WHEN OUT ON A LIMB.

HIS WORD IS TRUE, I KNOW.
WE CAN TRUST AND RELY ON IT
TO NEVER, NEVER RETURN VOID,
AS THE DEVIL, WE'LL OUTWIT.

MY ENEMY WOULD TELL ME LIES
AND LEAD MY THOUGHTS ASTRAY;
BUT I WILL TRUST GOD WITH MY HEART
AND THE WORD, OBEY.

I PRAY THAT I'LL BE BLAMELESS
WHEN I STAND AT JESUS FEET;
THEN I'LL KNOW, WITHOUT A DOUBT,
MY VICTORY IS COMPLETE.

## THE MOUNTAIN

FATHER, I HAVE STRUGGLED WITH
THIS MOUNTAIN IN MY WAY
FOR SUCH A VERY LONG, LONG TIME.
LET'S DEAL WITH IT TODAY!

IT'S HINDERED ME WHERE'ER I TURNED
AND MADE MY DAYS SO HARD;
NO MATTER WHAT I TRIED TO DO
THE WAY SEEMED TO BE BARRED.

YOU WORD SEEMS, OH, SO SIMPLE
UNTIL IT COMES TO DOING
AND THAT IS WHEN IT SEEMS
THE DEVIL STARTS HIS STEWING.

HE MIXES IN WITH OUR AFFAIRS,
THEN TRIES TO BRING CONFUSION
AND HE IS VERY HAPPY WHEN
WE CAN'T FIND A SOLUTION.

WE HAVE GOD'S PROMISE.
HE SAID HE WOULDN'T FORSAKE;
WITH US HE'LL ALWAYS BE
AND THE BATTLE, WE WILL TAKE.

NO MATTER WHAT THE MOUNTAIN BE,
HE SAID IT COULD BE MOVED.
IF WE WILL ONLY JUST BELIEVE,
OUR PATH MAY BE IMPROVED.

THEN, I WILL BE MUCH BETTER FIT
THE NEXT MOUNTAIN, THEN TO FACE
WITH A MUSTARD SEED OF FAITH,
IN HIM, TO RUN THE RACE.

SO IT SEEMS THAT I MUST TAKE
MY WILL TO DO HIS WORD
AND WHEN A WRONG'S BEEN MADE RIGHT;
I'VE DONE, AS WELL, AS HEARD.

## MY BLANKET

AS A CHILD, DID YOU EVER GO
UPSTAIRS TO FIND YOUR BED
AND GET YOUR FAVORITE BLANKET
TO PULL UP O'ER YOUR HEAD?

DID YOU SHUT OUT THE WORLD
AND CRY YOUR LITTLE TEARS
WHEN YOU HAD BEEN REJECTED
OR JUST TO HIDE FROM FEARS?

DID THIS, PERHAPS, GIVE TO YOU
A LITTLE TIME OF REST;
THEN HELPED TO GIVE YOU A SMILE
AND TRY TO BE YOUR BEST.

THE PRESSURES OF LIFE
LOOKING BACK SEEM SMALL;
BUT THEY WERE AN INTRODUCTION
TO THE GROWN UP WORLD, SO TALL.

NOW, IT IS NOT ADULT TO GO
TO FIND YOUR BLANKET, SOFT
AND RUN INTO YOUR BEDROOM
OR SOME COZY LITTLE LOFT.

AT TIMES WE CRY OURSELVES TO SLEEP
AND SHUT THE WORLD OUT;
BUT WE MUST TRY TO BE ADULT
NO MATTER WHAT IT'S ALL ABOUT.

LET ME TELL YOU GOD UNDERSTANDS.
HE WANTS US TO RUN TO HIM
AND TAKE THE BLANKET OF HIS LOVE
AND PULL IT TO THE CHIN.

AND AS WE WALK IN HIS LOVE
THROUGH PROBLEMS, BIG AND SMALL;
MEETING EACH CIRCUMSTANCE
HE'LL HELP US NOT TO FALL.

OUR ENEMY WOULD PUT US DOWN
AND TRY TO MAKE US BEND;
BUT THE BLANKET OF GOD'S LOVE
IS SUFFICIENT TO THE END.

## LIFE'S PATHWAY

SOMETIMES ALONG LIFE'S PATHWAY
WE NEED A HELPING HAND;
OR, JUST, A SMILE TO LIGHTEN A LOAD
WHEN THINGS DON'T GO AS PLANNED.

STRUGGLING THROUGH A CHALLENGE
WHEN THE WAY SEEMS SO OBSCURE
CAN SOMETIMES SEEM SO ENDLESS
JUST TRYING TO ENDURE.

DEALING WITH THE ANGER,
WHEN TRYING TO MAKE PEACE,
IS NOT ALWAYS EASY,
JUST PRAYING FOR RELEASE.

HOPING TO BE UNDERSTOOD
BY THOSE, WHO HAVE NO CLUE
OF HOPES AND DREAMS AND CIRCUMSTANCE
OR WHAT WE'RE GOING THROUGH.

COPING WITH LIFE'S PROBLEMS
AND DIRECTION FOR THE SOUL
WHILE GIVING LOVE TO EMPTY HEARTS,
IT'S HARD TO KEEP CONTROL.

SEARCHING FOR A TRUE LOVE
WHILE WE LIVE THIS LIFE
IS INDEED A CHALLENGE
TO GET THROUGH ALL THE STRIFE.

BUT GOD WILL BLESS OUR TRYING
HE'LL HELP US TO THE END;
STICKING CLOSER THAN A BROTHER
THROUGH THICK AND THIN, A FRIEND.

## THE LIGHT

ONE DAY I TOOK A LITTLE CANDLE
AND BURNED IT TO THE QUICK;
NOT FOR ANY PURPOSE
BUT FOR THE FUN OF IT.

AS I BURNED THAT CANDLE
IN MY HOUSE THAT NIGHT;
IT MADE EVERYTHING LOOK BETTER
WITH A SOFTENED LIGHT.

I PONDERED ON A LESSON
THE CANDLE HAD TO TEACH
AND FOUND AN UNDERSTANDING
MY SPIRIT, SOON, DID REACH.

I KNEW THE LORD, AS THE LIGHT
OUR SOULS HUNGER FOR.
BUT SOON, I SAW THE LIGHT WAS MORE;
IT WAS INDEED, A DOOR.

THE DOOR GAVE NEW HOPE AND PEACE
AS MY SPIRIT BEGAN TO SOAR;
IN THE LIGHT OF GOD'S LOVE
MY HEART DOES THIRST FOR MORE.

AND YET, I SAW ANOTHER THING
THAT WAS VERY CLEAR.
AS I DREW CLOSER TO THE FLAME;
THE WARMTH WAS VERY NEAR.

AS WE STEP INTO GOD'S LIGHT
EVEN MORE, WE FEEL HIS LOVE,
THE WARMTH OF HIS COMPASSION
AND HIS GOODNESS FROM ABOVE.

WHEN THE CANDLE HAD GONE OUT,
I SEARCHED FOR STILL ANOTHER
BECAUSE I NEEDED ALL THE LIGHT
THE DARKNESS FOR TO SMOTHER.

## BEYOND THE PAIN

I NEED TO GET BEYOND THE PAIN
OF THIS EMPTINESS, I FEEL;
WORKING OUT EMOTIONS
THAT ARE SO VERY REAL.

I CAN'T EXPLAIN THE DEPTH
OF ALL THAT RULES MY HEART.
I KNOW I MUST GO ON
AND MAKE A BRAND NEW START.

I HAVE GOD'S ASSURANCE.
HE WILL NOT LEAVE ME HERE
ALONE WITH THIS STRUGGLE.
HE'S PROMISED TO BE NEAR.

HE'LL BRING ME SAFELY THRU
THIS DARKNESS, I NOW FACE.
IN HIS PERFECT PEACE,
I'LL BE  IN HIS EMBRACE.

THE PLANS FOR TOMORROW
ARE WRITTEN BY HIS HAND.
WITH THE HOLY SPIRIT'S GUIDING,
TO DO JUST WHAT HE'D PLANNED.

PROVISIONS HAVE BEEN GRANTED
FOR NEEDS TO BE MET.
IF I JUST WALK WITH HIM,
I'LL HAVE NO REGRET.

HE WILL FILL MY NEEDS
AND, ALSO, MY DESIRES,
WHEN I DELIGHT IN THE LORD
JUST AS HE REQUIRES.

## TODAY

THE MOMENTS OF TODAY
ARE PRECIOUS IN GOD'S SIGHT.
BUT CAN WE SEE THE PROMISE
OF EACH MORNING LIGHT.

DO OUR MINDS MEANDER
TO ALL THE NEEDS THIS DAY;
OR DO WE STOP AND LISTEN
TO WHAT GOD HAS TO SAY?

THAT GENTLE VOICE OF HIS
GIVES DIRECTION TO OUR HEARTS.
WHEN WE TAKE THE TIME TO HEAR,
WISDOM, HE IMPARTS.

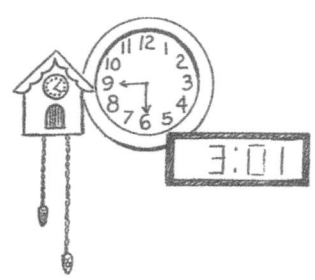

DO OUR THOUGHTS RUN TO TOMORROW
AND WHAT COULD BE;
WHILE BLINDED TO THE NEEDS TODAY
AND WHAT GOD WOULD HAVE US SEE?

ARE WE QUICK TO HEAR
AND THEN TO OBEY
OR DO THE CARES OF LIFE
CAUSE OUR THOUGHTS TO STRAY?

DOES GOD'S DESIRE FADE
AS WE CHOSE TO GO OUR WAY,
TRYING TO TAKE CONTROL
OR DO WE GIVE HIM TODAY?

I PRAY THAT WE WILL TREASURE
THE "NOW" THAT WE POSSESS.
TOMORROW NEVER COMES
IT'S TODAY THAT GOD WILL BLESS.

## ZAG-ZIG!

WHY DO PEOPLE ZAG
WHEN I THINK THEY SHOULD ZIG?
WHY IS LIFE SO COMPLICATED
AND PROBLEMS SEEM SO BIG?

WHY IS UNDERSTANDING
THE HARDEST THING TO DO?
I WONDER IF GOD REALLY CARES
WHEN I'M IN A STEW?

WHEN I THINK OF MY LIFE
AND THE CHOICES THAT I'VE MADE;
THAT GOD WAS WITH ME THROUGH IT ALL;
THEN THE WORRIES FADE.

HIS GRACE IS SUFFICIENT
OF THAT WE CAN BE SURE
WITH ALL THE BLESSINGS HE HAS GIVEN
AND KNOW THERE'S MORE IN STORE.

SO IF LIFE'S TWISTS AND TURNS
GO CONTRARY TO OUR DESIRES;
WE NEED TO ASK THE FATHER
JUST WHAT HE REQUIRES.

WE CAN KNOW THE ANSWER
IS JUST AROUND THE BEND;
AND AS WE WAIT THIS TRIAL OUT,
THEN, HIS GRACE HE'LL SEND.

## TOMORROW NEVER COMES

THE MOMENTS OF TODAY
ARE PRECIOUS IN GOD'S SIGHT
CAN WE SEE THE PROMISE
OF EACH MORNING LIGHT?

DOES THE MIND MEANDER
TO ALL THE NEEDS THIS DAY?
DO WE STOP AND LISTEN
TO WHAT HE HAS TO SAY?

CAN WE HEAR HIS GENTLE VOICE
GIVING DIRECTION TO OUR HEARTS;
TAKING TIME WITH HIM
AS EACH NEW DAY STARTS?

ARE WE QUICK TO HEAR
AND THEN TO OBEY?
OR DO THE CARES OF LIFE
ALLOW OUR THOUGHTS TO STRAY?

SOMETIMES, WE CHOSE OUR WILL
AND LET GOD'S DESIRE FADE;
AS WE HURRY ON OUR WAY,
THEN REGRET THE PATH WE MADE.

I PRAY THAT WE WILL TREASURE
THE "NOW" THAT WE POSSESS
FOR TOMORROW NEVER COMES.
IT'S TODAY THAT GOD WILL BLESS.

# TIME

A LETTER TO WRITE, A CARD FOR MY FRIEND
JUST WON'T GET DONE IF I WAIT.
FOR THE TIME TO BE RIGHT TO TACKLE A JOB;
THE CLOCK WILL ALWAYS BE LATE.

A MUCH NEEDED VISIT, A CALL ON THE PHONE
NEEDS MY FEET TO OBEY.
THOUGHTS COME EASY FOR HELPFUL DEEDS.
I'LL NOT THINK TOMORROW, BUT TODAY.

FOR A CAR WON'T GO TILL A KEY IS IN PLACE.
A CAKE WON'T GET BAKED WITHOUT HEAT.
DISHES WON'T GET DONE TILL WATER IS RUN
AND ANY JOB NEEDS MY HANDS AND MY FEET.

FAITH WITH OUT WORKS, I READ IN THE WORD
IS DEAD AND USELESS FOR GAIN.
WHAT NEEDS TO BE DONE THAT I FIND IN MY PATH
WILL SURELY BE WORTH THE PAIN.

SO. I'LL TACKLE EACH JOB THAT COMES MY WAY
AND PRAISE GOD WHEN IT IS DONE.
FOR EACH JOB, I'LL TRY TO DO MY BEST
AND NOT THINK ABOUT THE NEXT ONE.

## GOD'S LITTLE ONES

BLESSED ARE GOD'S LITTLE ONES
AS THEIR ANGELS ARE ON GUARD.
KEEPING THEM FROM HARM AND DOING GOD'S WILL,
SOMETIMES, IT SEEMS SO HARD.

FOR MAN LIVES ON A SINFUL EARTH
WITH DANGERS FAR AND WIDE
AND EVERYDAY SEEMS A TRIAL
TO KEEP US ON GOD'S SIDE.

AS CHILDREN GROW AND MEET LIFE'S TESTS
SOMETIMES THEY YIELD AND FALL
TO FEARFUL THOUGHTS AND DOING WRONG
NOT LISTENING TO GOD'S CALL.

IT'S THEN THEIR ANGELS DRAW THEM BACK
TO SEE WHAT THEY HAVE LOST.
THE PEACE OF GOD, THAT CAN'T BE BOUGHT,
IS WORTH WHATEVER COST.

SO GOD KEEPS SPEAKING TO THE HEART.
HE STRIVES FOR US, THE RIGHT.
TO BE OUR GOAL AND PAY THE PRICE;
THE REWARD IS WORTH THE FIGHT.

## THE DAUGHTER OF A KING

WHAT IF I'D BEEN BORN
THE DAUGHTER OF A KING
AND HAD MY PICK OF FURS AND JEWELS
AND ALMOST ANYTHING?

I'D HAVE LADIES JUST A-WAITING
TO GRANT MY EVERY WISH
AND TIME TO DO MY HEARTS DESIRE
AND HAVE MY FAVORITE DISH.

MENIAL TASKS WOULD NOT EXIST
FOR ANYONE SO ROYAL;
NO NEED TO THINK OF CLEANING UP
WITH SERVANTS, OH, SO LOYAL.

SOMEONE WOULD FEED THE CHILDREN
AND HUSH THEIR MANY CRIES,
WASH THEIR LITTLE BODIES
AND ANSWER ALL THEIR "WHYS?"

WOULD IT BE ALL I'D DREAMED
OR WOULD I MISS THE FEEL
OF DOING ALL THE MANY THINGS
THAT MAKE A FAMILY REAL?

NOW, I WILL BE SO THANKFUL
FOR EACH DIRTY DISH AND PAN
AND THE HEAP OF DIRTY CLOTHES.
THEY MUST BE IN GOD'S PLAN.

I'LL THANK GOD FOR EACH CHILD'S CRY
AND MEALS TO COOK AND ALL;
KNOWING, I AM IN GOD'S WILL
AND ANSWERING HIS 'CALL.'

## MORNING LIGHT

THE SUN PEAKS OVER THE TREETOPS,
SOON TO PARCH THE FOG AND THE DEW;
GOD'S PROMISE THAT HE'S IN HIS HEAVEN
IS HIS MERCY, TO ME BORN A-NEW.

MY MIND IS FLOODED WITH THOUGHTS DIVINE
WHILE PROBLEMS OF LIFE SEEM SMALL;
AND IN THE LIGHT OF OUR SAVIOR'S LOVE
MY SPIRIT, ONLY, MUST CALL.

MY NEEDS, HE SAID HE WOULD PROVIDE;
I HAVE, ONLY TO ASK.
LOVE FOR HIS CHILD WILL NEVER END
IT SEEMS, TO ME SUCH A TASK.

MANY TIMES, NOT LOVABLE, I KNOW FULL WELL
AS THE PRESSURES OF LIFE COME TO BEAR;
EMOTIONS RISE AS MY MIND WONDERS ON
AND THE LIGHT, HE BRINGS, SHOWS HIS CARE.

HE CARES WHERE MY PATH LEADS.
HE UNDERSTANDS MY CRY!
THE ANSWER'S PROVIDED IF I ONLY STOP
AND CEASE THE WHEN AND THE WHY.

FOR 'THE WHEN' IS GOD'S TIMING,
'THE WHY' IS HIS GRACE;
FOR HE IS THE ANSWER
IN WHATEVER I FACE.

## A LITTLE IS BETTER THAN NOTHING

A LITTLE IS BETTER THAN NOTHING
WHEN STARTING A TASK IN MY WAY.
IF THE TASK SEEMS TOO BIG TO IMAGINE,
"A LITTLE BIT, NOW," I WILL SAY.

IF A REASON, I SEEK TO GIVE ME A START
AS MY FEET DRAG TO ANSWER A CALL.
BEGINNING A JOB WILL SHORTEN THE LOAD,
THE MOUNTAIN, THEN WON'T SEEM SO TALL.

A LETTER TO WRITE OR A CARD FOR MY FRIEND
JUST WON'T GET DONE IF I WAIT.
FOR THE TIME TO BE RIGHT TO TACKLE THE JOB,
THE CLOCK WILL ALWAYS BE LATE.

A MUCH NEEDED VISIT OR A CALL ON THE PHONE
NEEDS MY FEET TO OBEY.
THOUGHTS COME EASY FOR HELPFUL DEEDS;
BUT, I MUST MAKE THE WAY.

GOD WILL HELP ME IF I ASK.
HE NEEDS MY HANDS, FEET AND MIND.
IF I TAKE THE FIRST STEP AND FOLLOW THROUGH;
HE'LL HELP ME EVERY TIME.

## TIDES

THE TIDES ARE EVER CONSTANT,
COMING MORNING, NOON AND NIGHT;
ETCHING AT THE SHORELINE,
HARD AND ANGRY, SOFT AND LIGHT.

LIKE THE TIDES OF OUR LIFETIME,
SOMETIMES HAPPY, SOMETIMES SAD;
COME AS SURE AS THE SUNRISE,
WHETHER GOOD OR WHETHER BAD.

JOYING IN GOD'S CREATION,
BREATHING THE TRANQUILITY,
SETTLING A RESTLESS SPIRIT,
AND ACCEPTING WHAT WILL BE.

HE IS IN OUR YESTERDAYS
AND TOMORROW, HE WILL GUIDE.
HE'LL MAKE US STRONG THROUGH TRIALS,
WHILE IN HIM WE ABIDE.

## GOD'S PRESENCE AT THE SHORE

GOD'S PRESENCE IS SO NEAR
WHILE SITTING BY THE SEA.
THE RHYTHM OF THE WAVES
SEEM TO MAKE THE DOLDRUMS FLEE.

WARM AND GENTLE BREEZES
CALM THE TROUBLED MIND.
IT ALWAYS FEELS SO GOOD
TO SIT AND JUST - UNWIND!

SEAGULLS DODGING FOR SOME FOOD.
SUNBEAMS DANCING ON THE WAVES.
THE SERENITY  IT GIVES,
MY SPIRIT REALLY CRAVES.

YOU CAN'T GET  IN A BOTTLE
THE PEACE THAT SETTLES IN;
BY LETTING  GOD'S CREATION
BRING HIS JOY WITHIN.

AND WHEN LIFE'S STORMS ARISE
AS THEY ALWAYS WILL
MEMORY OF THESE SPECIAL TIMES
HELPS MY HEART TO STILL.

## SEEDS

WHEN YOU ARISE IN THE EARLY MORN
AND THINK WHAT YOUR DAY MIGHT HOLD;
WHAT KIND OF ROAD YOUR DAY MIGHT BE
AS THOSE TWENTY-FOUR HOURS ENFOLD.

REMEMBER GOD, IN HIS INFINITE LOVE,
PLANNED TIME JUST FOR YOU.
THIS DAY IS ONE, NEVER SEEN BEFORE.
IT'S BLESSINGS ARE BRAND NEW.

AS YOU PONDER ABOUT THE WAY
YOUR PATH MIGHT SEEM TO GO;
KNOW GOOD THINGS WILL COME ALONG,
AS MANY SEEDS, YOU'LL SOW.

THEY COULD BE SEEDS OF KINDNESS
OR COMFORT FOR A FRIEND,
A LISTENING EAR, A CARING SMILE,
A THOUGHTFUL LETTER, FOR TO SEND.

THESE SEEDS MIGHT BE RETURNED
WHEN YOU NEED A HELPING HAND;
AND THINGS, JUST, HAVEN'T GONE
EXACTLY AS YOU'D PLANNED.

THINGS WOULD BE MUCH BETTER
AS YOUR THOUGHTS STAY ON HIM;
THEN YOUR PATH WOULD NOT BE TURNED
BY EVERY LITTLE WHIM.

YOU KNOW HIS WAYS ARE BEST
AND THAT HE HAS THE KEY
OF HOW TO WALK YOUR ROAD TODAY
SO YOUR SPIRIT WILL BE FREE.

## HELP ME

HELP ME BE CONTENT, LORD,
WITH THE THINGS THAT YOU PROVIDE.
THANK YOU FOR ALL YOU'VE GIVEN;
FORGIVE ME FOR MY PRIDE.

LET ME NOT LOOK AT OTHERS
FOR WHAT THEY DO POSSESS
BUT SHOW ME ALL THE VALUE
OF WHICH I HAVE BEEN BLESSED.

I NEED TO MAKE THE TIME
YOU'VE GIVEN FOR TODAY
BE USED FOR YOUR GLORY
NOT, JUST, STUBBLE AND HAY.

GRANT ME EYES TO SEE THE NEEDS
OF ONES PUT IN MY LIFE.
YOUR EARS TO HEAR THE CRIES
OF HEARTACHES AND STRIFE.

HELP ME TO KNOW THE WAY
YOU WANT MY STEPS TO GO;
SO WHEN THE DAY IS DONE,
FULFILLMENT, I WILL KNOW.

## NO REGRETS

IN OUR WALK WITH GOD,
WE PRAY HE LEADS OUR STEPS;
WHEN WE REACH THE GOAL
THAT THERE ARE NO REGRETS.

TO HIS VOICE, WE TRY TO LISTEN
AND OBEY HIS EVERY CALL,
WALK IN HIS BLESSING
AND PRAY WE DO NOT FALL.

HE SAID HE'D NEVER LEAVE US
TO RUN THIS RACE ALONE.
HE KNOWS OUR NAME AND ADDRESS
AND DOESN'T NEED A PHONE.

WE'VE GOT A HOLY ROAD MAP
TO CHART US ON OUR WAY.
WE NEED TO READ AND LIVE IT
AND LET GOD HAVE HIS SAY.

HIS WORD IS GIVEN FREELY
AND WISDOM WHEN WE ASK.
IT'S MORE THAN WHAT WE NEED
TO COMPLETE OUR TASK.

WHEN WE GET TO HEAVEN
WE'LL SEE WITH BRAND NEW EYES.
THROUGH UPS AND DOWNS, INS AND OUTS,
HE ALWAYS HEARD OUR CRIES.

## WHAT ARE YOU SAYING

WHAT ARE YOU SAYING
TO MY HEART TODAY?
WHAT WOULD YOU SPEAK
TO ME, I PRAY?

WHERE SHOULD I GO
OBEYING YOUR VOICE?
WHAT IS YOUR PURPOSE?
HELP ME MAKE THE RIGHT CHOICE.

WHEN IS THE RIGHT TIME?
YOUR WILL, PLEASE, MAKE CLEAR;
THE TIMING MAKE PERFECT,
YOUR VOICE, HELP ME HEAR.

HOW DO I GIVE YOU
ALL THAT YOU ASK?
GOD GIVE ME DIRECTION
AND, PLEASE, MAKE IT FAST!

MY EYES NEED TO BE
FOCUSED ON YOU;
NOT SEEING THE BAD
BUT, ONLY WHAT'S TRUE.

I NEED YOUR PERSPECTIVE
IN FACING EACH DAY;
AS EACH CHALLENGE, I MEET
REMIND ME TO PRAY.

## LET GOD

WHAT DOES "LET GOD" REALLY MEAN?
HOW CAN I TRULY KNOW
WHEN I HOLD ALL THESE HURTS
FROM HIM, SO LOVE CAN'T FLOW?

THINGS THAT STAND IN MY WAY
MUST NO LONGER HAVE CONTROL;
TO KEEP ME FROM GOD'S PRESENCE,
HOLDING ME FROM BEING WHOLE.

WHAT IS THE KEY THAT I MUST SEE,
MY FOE'S POWER, TO REMOVE?
WHERE DO I FIND THE ANSWER,
THIS CHALLENGE TO IMPROVE?

FORGIVENESS, GOD COMMANDS,
NO MATTER WHAT WRONG'S BEEN DONE
IT'S THE SOLUTION THAT I SEEK,
FOR ME, THE ONLY ONE.

FORGETTING'S THEN THE ROADBLOCK
FOR FINDING A RELEASE
AND HAVE WHAT ONLY GOD GIVES,
WHAT I NEED, A PERFECT PEACE.

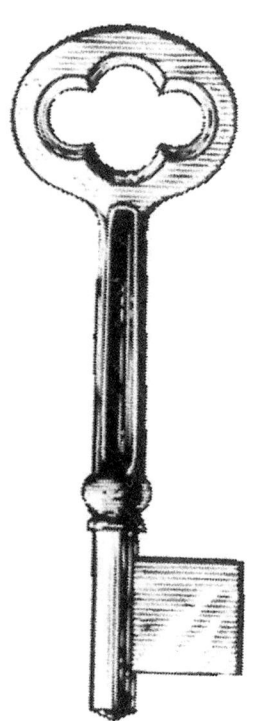

ONE MORE THING I MUST DO
IF GOD'S PEACE HASN'T COME,
I KNOW I MUST FORGIVE
THE WRONG THAT'S BEEN DONE.

GOD'S PERSPECTIVE FOR MY EYES
TO SEE BEYOND THE PAIN
IS WHAT I NEED FOR VICTORY;
IT'S THERE FOR ME TO CLAIM.

THEN, I'LL JOURNEY ONWARD,
LOOKING UP AND NEVER BACK
TO THE STUFF THAT KEPT ME
FROM STAYING ON GOD'S TRACK.

## HOLY SPIRIT, BE MY GUIDE

HOLY SPIRIT, BE MY GUIDE.
WALK WITH ME TODAY.
SHOW ME WHAT I NEED TO SEE.
HELP THIS LUMP OF CLAY.

KEEP MY THOUGHTS PURE AND TRUE,
FAULTS OF OTHERS, NOT TO SEE.
BUT SENSING THEIR POTENTIAL
AND JUST, WHAT THEY CAN BE.

GIVE ME A PLAN OF ACTION
SO THIS DAY WILL BE WORTHWHILE;
NO MATTER WHAT LIES AHEAD
I CAN FACE IT WITH A SMILE.

I KNOW YOU ARE WITH ME
AND WILL GIVE ME WHAT I NEED;
THE STRENGTH TO DO WHAT'S RIGHT
AS YOU GENTLY LEAD.

HOLY SPIRIT, MAKE THE WORD
LIVING AND ALIVE IN ME.
SPEAK TO ME LOUD AND CLEAR.
GIVE ME WORDS THAT FREE.

OPEN UP MY HEART TODAY
TO WHAT I NEED TO KNOW;
RHEMA FOR MY HUNGRY SOUL
GIVE WORDS OF LIFE TO GROW.

LIGHT YOUR FIRE IN MY HEART
STRENGTH TO MEET THE DAY,
HOPE TO KNOW YOU ARE THERE
AND YOU'LL NEVER GO AWAY.

GIVE ME YOUR EYES TO SEE
WHERE I NEED TO GO;
TO DO THE TASKS YOU ORDAIN
YOUR WILL, FOR ME, PLEASE SHOW.

## HOPE

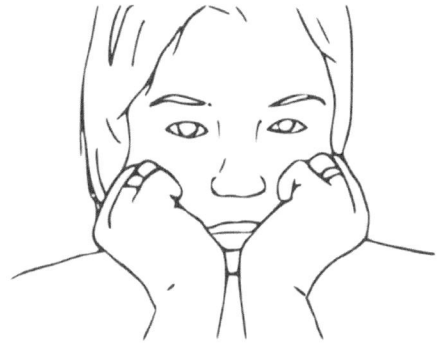

GOD'S GRACE IS BETTER SEEN
ON A CLOUDY DAY.
HIS LOVE COMES SWEETER STILL
WHEN MUDDIER HAS BEEN OUR WAY.

THE HOPE THAT HE WILL SEND
TO LIGHTEN UP OUR LOAD;
SEEMS A GREATER BLESSING
AFTER WALKING A ROUGHER ROAD.

IF STORM CLOUDS DIDN'T GATHER
AND TROUBLES WEIGH US DOWN;
THE RAINBOWS OF OUR LIFE
WOULD NEVER COME AROUND.

THE SUNBEAMS WOULDN'T SHINE
FOR US, QUITE, SO BRIGHT;
IF WE DIDN'T ENDURE
A LONG AND DISMAL NIGHT.

BUT GOD WILL SEND US NEW HOPE.
IT'S THE WAITING THAT'S SO HARD.
DOUBTING SEEMS TO PLAGUE US,
AS OUR HEARTS, WE GUARD.

TIME IS THE CULPRIT
AS WE SEEK HIS GRACE.
HE HAS THE ANSWER
WHEN WE SEEK HIS FACE.

35

## IS THERE SOMEONE CRYING?

IS THERE SOMEONE CRYING
MAYBE FAR AWAY
TRYING TO STAY STRONG,
EVEN THIS VERY DAY?

IS SOMEONE HELD IN BONDAGE
THEIR LIFE, IN JEOPARDY
HELD CAPTIVE FOR BELIEVING;
THE NEED, WE JUST, MUST SEE?

THE NEED'S TO SAY A PRAYER
FOR A SISTER IN DISTRESS.
COULD WE CALL ON ANGELS
TO HELP HER MEET HER TEST?

IS THERE A DOWNCAST BROTHER
JUST TRYING TO HANG ON;
IN A DREARY, DIRTY CELL
PRAYING FOR THE DAWN?

HOW CAN WE FORGET OUR FAMILY,
CRYING OUT IN DEEP DESPAIR;
WHEN OUR PRAYERS COULD ANSWER
THE PLIGHT OF A PRECIOUS ONE, SOMEWHERE?

THEIR LIFE MAY SOON BE TAKEN
BUT WE CAN BE A PART
OF PRAYING FOR THEIR STRENGTH
SO THEY DO NOT LOSE HEART.

GOD, GIVE THEM THE STRENGTH
THEIR VALLEY, TO WALK THROUGH
AND BE A LIGHT FOR JESUS
EVEN, TO DEATH, BE TRUE.

AND WHEN WE GET TO HEAVEN
WHERE THERE IS NO MORE FEAR;
WE'LL MEET THE ONES WE PRAYED FOR,
THAT GOD HOLDS, OH SO DEAR.

## BUTTERFLY

A SIGN OF NEW LIFE,
IN A BUTTERFLY.
A SAGA IS TOLD
AS THEIR WINGS TESTIFY.

PLANTS, THAT ARE EATEN,
AND HONEY SO SWEET
ARE MAGNIFIED BEAUTY,
IN THEIR COLORS, COMPLETE.

IF THEY EAT SOUR PLANTS,
IT'S DEFENSE FOR THE WORM.
GOD'S PLAN FOR THE CREATURE
CAUSES IT'S ENEMIES TO TURN.

SO THE SWEET AND THE SOUR
AS A  WORM, THEN INGESTS;
IS PART OF THE  MAKE-UP
FOR IT'S LIFE, GOD INVESTS.

WE, TOO, ARE A TOTAL
OF TIMES, GOOD AND BAD;
OUR LIVES, A WITNESS
DAYS, JOYFUL AND SAD.

HE'LL USE ALL WE GIVE
FOR GOOD, TO OTHER'S SHOW.
THROUGH THE COLORS OF OUR LIVES
WE CAN HAVE A SPECIAL GLOW.

## WORDS

"THANK YOU," ARE TWO SIMPLE WORDS
WHEN SAID FROM THE HEART.
THEY GIVE A SPECIAL FEELING
AND ARE WORDS THAT CAN'T BE BOUGHT.

IT'S A GIFT SPOKEN TO SOMEONE
THAT SAW THERE WAS A NEED
AND GAVE A LITTLE OF THEMSELVES
BY PLANTING A LOVE SEED.

GOD SAID THAT IT IS BETTER
TO GIVE THAN TO RECEIVE.
HE'S PLEASED WE'VE CARED ENOUGH.
WE REALLY MUST BELIEVE.

"I'M SORRY," ALSO IS A GIFT,
SOMETIMES, HARD TO SAY.
IT CAN CHANGE THE ATMOSPHERE
AND TURN AROUND A DAY.

BUT, "PLEASE FORGIVE ME,"IS A KEY
THAT, "I'M SORRY," CANNOT HOLD.
IT GIVES RELEASE TO THE SOUL,
WORTH MUCH MORE THAN GOLD.

IT'S GOOD TO REAP THE BENEFITS
OF KEEPING OUR SLATES CLEAN;
TO SAY THE WORDS THAT MEAN SO MUCH
IS A BLESSING, WE CAN GLEAN.

**I'm Sorry!**

**Please
Forgive
Me!**

## FORGIVENESS

FORGIVENESS IS THE ANSWER
TO OFFENCES PRESENT, FUTURE, PAST.
THO IT BE GREAT OR LITTLE,
WE CAN HAVE PEACE AT LAST.

JUST TO SPEAK THE WORDS
SEEMS, OFTEN TIMES, SO HARD;
TO BE VULNERABLE FOR OTHERS
AND LET DOWN OUR GUARD.

WITH MAN'S NATURE, WE MUST DEAL
PROTECTIVE, THOUGH WE BE;
TO HOLD ON TO THINGS THAT HURT,
WHEN GOD WANTS US TO BE FREE.

YOU SEE, IT IS SO SIMPLE.
THE FORMULA IS SO PLAIN;
RELEASING THE INJUSTICE,
THE SOURCE OF THE PAIN.

SO WHEN WE ASK FORGIVENESS;
GOD WILL GIVE US GRACE.
HE'LL HEAL THE BROKEN HEARTED
AND SINS COMMITTED, HE'LL ERASE.

## HOPES AND DREAMS

SHATTERED HOPES AND DREAMS,
UNSPOKEN WORDS OF LOVE
CRY HEALING FOR THE SOUL
AND COMFORT FROM ABOVE.

WE'VE LET STRESS AND HEARTACHE
AND CIRCUMSTANCES, DEEP;
PULL OUR SPIRITS DOWN
THEN THEY STEAL OUR SLEEP.

UNSPOKEN WORDS OF CARING,
BROKEN PROMISES CRY OUT,
WAITING FOR FORGIVENESS
AND SURRENDER OF THE HEART.

'IF ONLY,' CALLS SO LOUDLY,
'MAYBE IF,' TRIES TO BE HEARD;
BUT HEAVEN WANTS TO HEAR
US UTTER JUST A WORD.

FORGIVE, FORGET, LIVE FREELY,
WHY IS IT SO HARD
TO GIVE UP ALL THE HURT AND PAIN
AND JUST LET DOWN OUR GUARD?

GOD'S WAITING JUST TO HEAR
OUR VOICE TO HEAVEN RAISE.
THEN BLESSINGS, WE WILL KNOW
AND ANGELS, WITH US PRAISE.

## ANGELS FROM GLORY

ANGELS FROM GLORY,
ON MISSIONS HERE ARE SENT;
PROVIDING THEIR PROTECTION
FROM OUR FOES INTENT.

OF THE EVIL ONE'S DEVICES,
UNSUSPECTING, THOUGH WE BE;
ANGELS ARE ALWAYS ON ALERT,
THERE TO KEEP US FREE.

HOW MANY TIMES
HAVE DANGER'S BEEN AVERTED;
THE TIMES OUR ANGELS
THE ENEMY'S REVERTED.

AS WE STRUGGLE IN THIS LIFE
GOD'S LOVE NEVER FALTERS.
YESTERDAY, TODAY, FOREVER;
HIS CARE NEVER ALTERS.

NO MATTER WHERE OUR PATHS MAY GO
HE WILL NEVER LEAVE;
HIS PROMISES, HIS GUARANTEE
OUR PART'S TO BELIEVE.

BELIEVE WHAT HE'S PROVIDED
SALVATION, STRONG AND TRUE;
ANGELS BRING HIS MESSAGE
AND HELP TO SEE US THROUGH.

41

## A BEAUTIFUL MORNING

A BEAUTIFUL MORNING SUNRISE,
MAJESTIC MOUNTAINS HIGH,
LIFT MY SOUL HEAVENWARD;
AS I BREATHE A SIGH.

TAKING IN GOD'S CREATION,
MARVELING AT THE SIGHT,
ALLOWING THOUGHTS OF TURMOIL,
OF LIFE TO TAKE THEIR FLIGHT.

A RIPPLING STREAM,
A BIRD CALLING TO ITS MATE,
GOD'S PRESENCE FILLS THE AIR,
AS WITH HIM, I COMMUNICATE.

FINDING A NEW PERSPECTIVE,
THE PEACE OF GOD DESCENDS.
TRUSTING IN HIS WORD,
MY LIFE ON HIM DEPENDS.

## THANKFUL

I'M THANKFUL FOR THE LITTLE THINGS
THAT HELP TO MAKE MY DAY;
A HAPPY FACE, A BUTTERFLY,
WATCHING CHILDREN PLAY.

IT'S GOOD TO THINK OF BLESSINGS,
NOT DWELLING ON OUR PAIN;
BUT PULLING BACK THE CLOUDS
TO THE SUNSHINE THROUGH THE RAIN.

WHEN PROBLEMS DO SURROUND
AND MERCY SEEMS TO HIDE;
REMEMBER GOD'S NOT GONE,
HE'S RIGHT THERE BY YOUR SIDE.

MANY DISAPPOINTMENTS
AND THE CARES OF LIFE
CROWD THE HEART WITH SORROW
AND FILL SOME DAYS WITH STRIFE.

STILL, I HAVE AN ASSURANCE,
NO MATTER WHAT THE NEED
THAT GOD HEARS MY PETITION
AND WANTS ME TO SUCCEED.

## THE BLOOD

I NEED TO PLEAD THE BLOOD
OVER WHAT IS MINE;
WHAT GOD HAS GIVEN
FOR THIS SPACE IN TIME.

THE POWER GOD'S ALLOTTED
BY THE SACRIFICE WAS PAID;
OF HIS SON ON THE CROSS
WHEN DOWN, HIS LIFE, HE LAID.

THAT BLOOD, SO PRECIOUS,
WHEN HIS WORDS WE SPEAK;
FLOWS OVER OUR LIVES AND
GIVES STRENGTH TO THE WEAK.

HEALING IS GRANTED
WHEN THE BLOOD IS APPLIED.
OUR LORD'S PAID THE PRICE
UNDER HIS WINGS, WE CAN HIDE.

NO NEED TO STRUGGLE
AS WE OFTEN DO.
OUR TROUBLES IN LIFE
HE ALREADY KNEW.

**IN YOUR PRESENCE**

THE LONGING OF MY HEART
IS TO BE IN YOUR EMBRACE,
FEELING YOUR PRESENCE,
RESTING IN YOUR GRACE.

I WANT TO FEEL YOUR COMPASSION,
THE DEPTH OF LOVE, TO KNOW;
AS YOU TOUCH MY VERY SOUL,
BATHING IN THE HEAVENLY GLOW.

HELP ME TO SEE YOUR MERCY
AS MY SINS YOU FORGIVE,
HEAR THE CRY OF MY HEART,
VICTORIOUSLY TO LIVE.

LIVING WATER, POUR ON ME,
ANOINTING FROM YOUR HAND.
IMMERSE ME IN YOUR PRESENCE
AND HELP ME TO STAND.

I NEED TO KNOW YOU BETTER,
TO FEEL YOUR LOVING CARE
AND KNOW THAT YOU ARE WITH ME,
THE ANSWER TO MY PRAYER.

## GLORY SHOWERS

I STAND ON THE THRESHOLD
OF HEAVEN AND EARTH
SEEKING THE PEACE
FOR WHICH, I'VE BEEN BIRTHED.

AS I STEP IN THE THRONE ROOM
AND GAZE AT ITS SPLENDER
I'M HUMBLED BEFORE GOD
IN UTTER SURRENDER.

RAINBOW DROPLETS FALL,
THE COLORS, FASCINATING,
IRIDESCENT GLORY,
OF GOD'S WORD, CREATING.

AS THEY PIERCE AND PENETRATE
THIS SEEKING HEART OF MINE
DOUBT AND FEAR FLEE AWAY.
IT IS BY GOD'S DESIGN.

GLORY SHOWERS, FILLED WITH LOVE
MY BEING SATURATES.
DROPLETS OF COMPASSION,
MY HUNGRY HEART, AWAITS.

ETERNITY STRETCHES ON.
TIME, FOR ME, STANDS STILL.
HIS PEACE INVADES MY BEING
FROM HIS HOLY HILL.

I KNOW THIS GIFT HAS BEEN GIVEN
FOR  MORE THAN JUST MY JOY;
IT'S MEANT FOR ONES, WHO NEED HIS LOVE
THOSE, WHO SATAN WOULD DESTROY.

MAY THIS BLESSING NEVER CEASE
AS I JOURNEY ON MY WAY,
ALWAYS GIVING ME HIS LOVE
EACH AND EVERY DAY.

## JESUS IS COMING

JESUS IS COMING,
IT MAY BE REAL SOON;
BE READY, LOOK UPWARD
MORN, NIGHT OR NOON.

HE'S WAITING FOR SOMEONE.
PERHAPS, IT IS YOU
TO GET READY TO MEET HIM
AND A HEART, RENEW.

THE WORD HAS BEEN GIVEN
BY THE FATHER ABOVE
AS ANGELS IN GLORY
SURROUND US WITH LOVE.

THE PRICE HAS BEEN PAID
FOR ALL WHO'LL BELIEVE
THAT COME TO THE CROSS
AND CHRIST RECEIVE.

HE'S DONE IT ALL
THE GIFT, IT IS FREE.
SALVATION FROM SIN
AND TO LIVE ETERNALLY.

SO DON'T WASTE THE TIME.
ANSWER THE CALL
OF HIS LOVE EXTENDED
WITH FORGIVENESS FOR ALL.

47

Made in the USA
Lexington, KY
24 April 2016